This book belon

_____

This book is dedicated to my children - Mikey, Kobe, and Jojo.

Paperback ISBN: 978-1-63731-323-7
Hardcover ISBN: 978-1-63731-325-1
eBook ISBN: 978-1-63731-324-4

Printed and bound in the USA.
NinjaLifeHacks.tv

Ninja Life Hacks™

St. Patrick's Day Race

By Mary Nhin

When St. Patrick's Day is nearing,
Ninjas get excited!
The St. Patrick's Day race is on again,
Which makes us **SO** delighted!

The race is a grand tradition.
It's held over 400 yards.
I think that perhaps this year,
A win is in the cards.

Some ninjas wait to start training,
Others dive right in.
But I think a four-leaf clover,
Will help me achieve a win!

So I go looking high and low,
Even when it's raining.
But while I'm searching, other ninjas,
Continue with their training.

A rainbow?! Yes!! That always means,
A four-leaf clover's near.
Come on, I can do it!
That magic clover **MUST** be here!

But no. It's not. Nothing at all,
Except a pot of gold,
And a laughing Leprechaun,
Who's 200 years old!

"Well, well, well," the Leprechaun says,
"You look a bit dumbstruck."
"What will I do?" I cry,
"How will I win without luck?"

The Leprechaun flashes a toothy grin,
His golden teeth aglow.
"Gritty Ninja," he quietly says,
"There's something you should know."

"I'm 200 years old, yes, it's true,
And I'm lucky every day.
The harder I work, the luckier I get,
That's the Leprechaun way."

"So run, Gritty Ninja, run, run, run!
I know there's luck in you.
All you need to do is work hard,
Now show what you can do!"

So I run and sprint,
Up and down the rainbow.
Training hard, so at race time,
I know I'm good to go!

Speaking of go ... **GO, NINJAS! GO!**
The starting gun is fired.
After two laps, ninjas with clovers
Are already feeling tired.

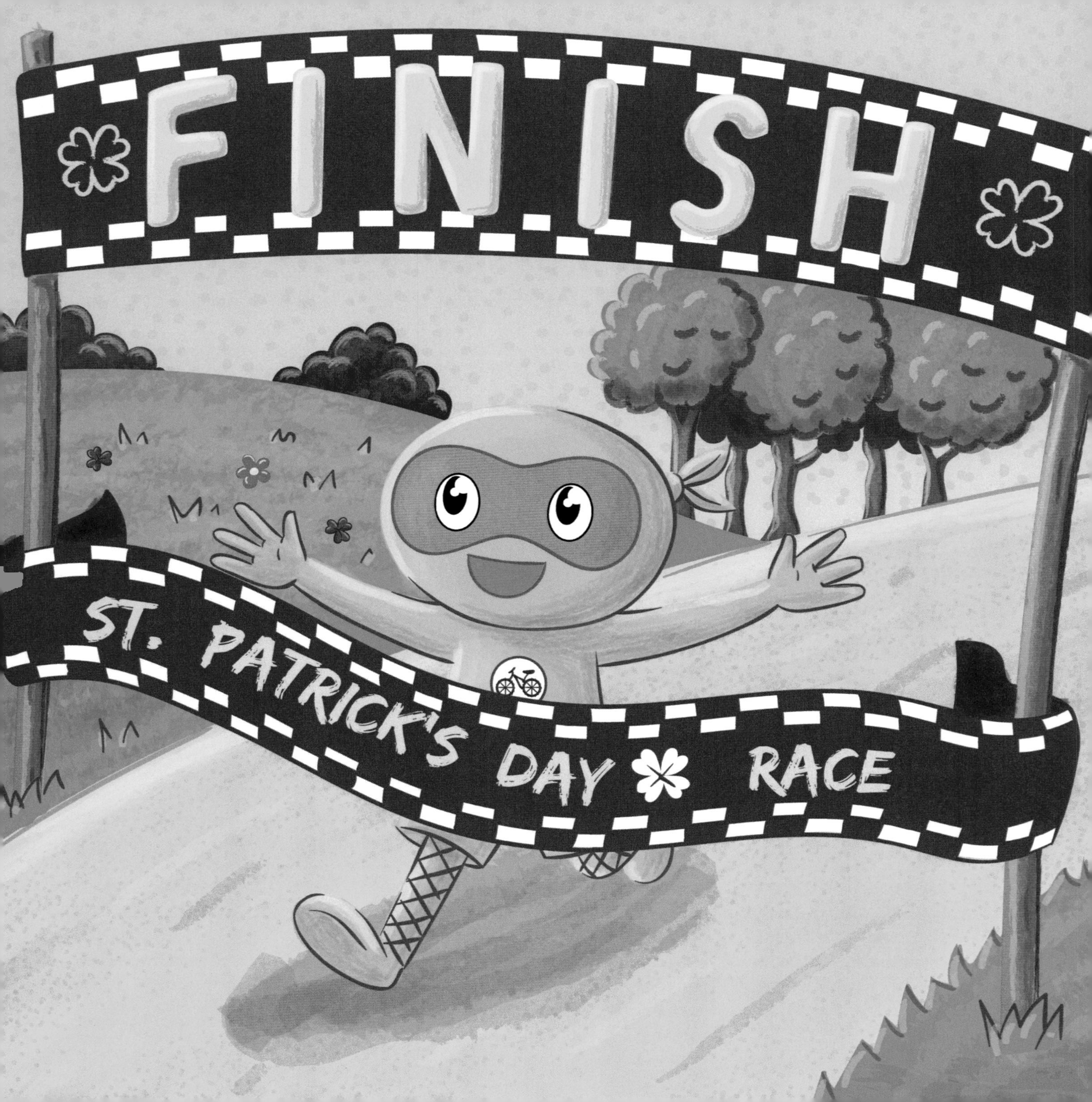
FINISH
ST. PATRICK'S DAY RACE

I tap into my mental strength.
And with one final burst,
I focus on breathing and...
Cross the finish line first.

You may not always have good luck,
Or ace every difficult test.
But you're a winner if, like me,
You work hard and do your best.

Made in the USA
Las Vegas, NV
06 March 2024

86774733R00021